Nevermore

Nevermore

The Raven

VISIONS IN POETRY

EDGAR ALLAN POE

The Raven

WITH ILLUSTRATIONS BY

RYAN PRICE

KCP POETRY

An Imprint of Kids Can Press

Once upon a midnight dreary,
   while I pondered, weak and weary,
Over many a quaint and curious volume
   of forgotten lore,

BIR

While I nodded, nearly napping,
    suddenly there came a tapping,
As of some one gently rapping,
    rapping at my chamber door.
"'Tis some visiter," I muttered,
    "tapping at my chamber door —
        Only this, and nothing more."

Ah, distinctly I remember it was in
    the bleak December,
And each separate dying ember
    wrought its ghost upon the floor.
Eagerly I wished the morrow;
    — vainly I had tried to borrow
From my books surcease of sorrow
    — sorrow for the lost Lenore —

For the rare and radiant maiden
whom the angels name Lenore —

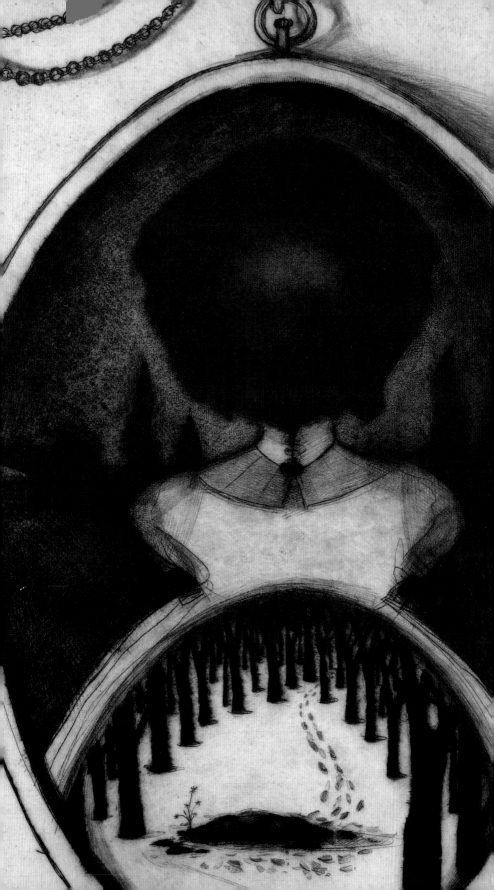

Nameless here for evermore.

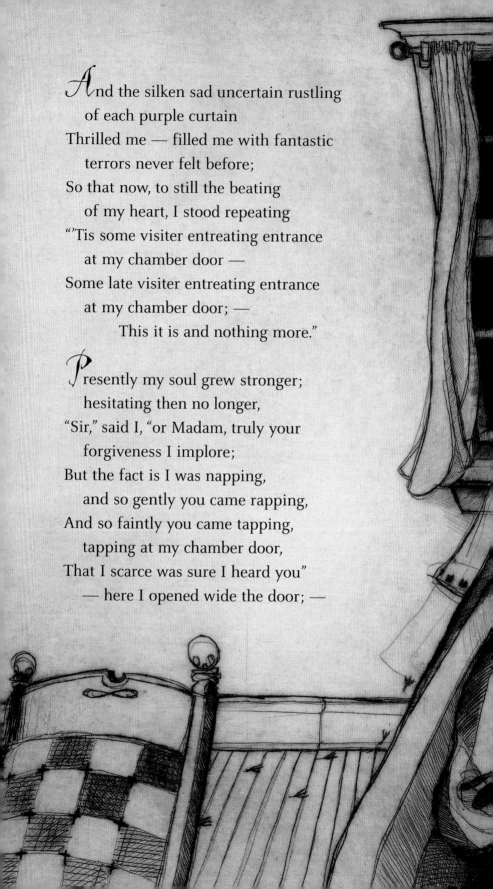

And the silken sad uncertain rustling
   of each purple curtain
Thrilled me — filled me with fantastic
   terrors never felt before;
So that now, to still the beating
   of my heart, I stood repeating
"'Tis some visiter entreating entrance
   at my chamber door —
Some late visiter entreating entrance
   at my chamber door; —
      This it is and nothing more."

Presently my soul grew stronger;
   hesitating then no longer,
"Sir," said I, "or Madam, truly your
   forgiveness I implore;
But the fact is I was napping,
   and so gently you came rapping,
And so faintly you came tapping,
   tapping at my chamber door,
That I scarce was sure I heard you"
   — here I opened wide the door; —

Darkness there,
and nothing more.

*D*eep into that darkness peering,
  long I stood there wondering, fearing,
Doubting, dreaming dreams no mortal
  ever dared to dream before;
But the silence was unbroken,
  and the darkness gave no token,
And the only word there spoken
  was the whispered word, "Lenore!"
This *I* whispered, and an echo
  murmured back the word, "Lenore!"
    Merely this, and nothing more.

*T*hen into the chamber turning,
  all my soul within me burning,
Soon I heard again a tapping
  somewhat louder than before.
"Surely," said I, "surely that is
  something at my window lattice;
Let me see, then, what thereat is,
  and this mystery explore —
Let my heart be still a moment
  and this mystery explore; —
    'Tis the wind,
      and nothing more!"

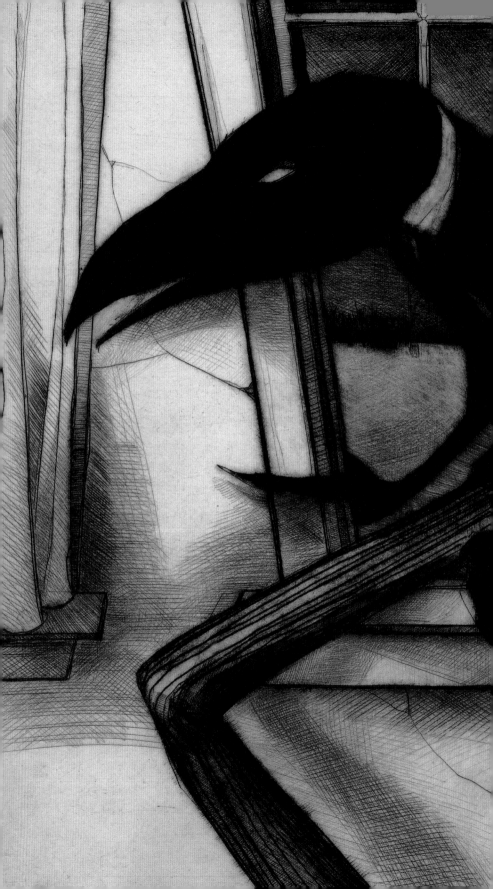

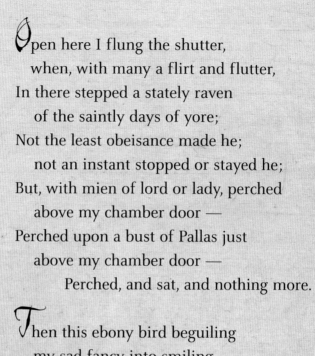

Open here I flung the shutter,
    when, with many a flirt and flutter,
In there stepped a stately raven
    of the saintly days of yore;
Not the least obeisance made he;
    not an instant stopped or stayed he;
But, with mien of lord or lady, perched
    above my chamber door —
Perched upon a bust of Pallas just
    above my chamber door —
        Perched, and sat, and nothing more.

Then this ebony bird beguiling
    my sad fancy into smiling,
By the grave and stern decorum
    of the countenance it wore,
"Though thy crest be shorn and shaven,
    thou," I said, "art sure no craven,
Ghastly grim and ancient raven
    wandering from the Nightly shore —
Tell me what thy lordly name is on
    the Night's Plutonian shore!"

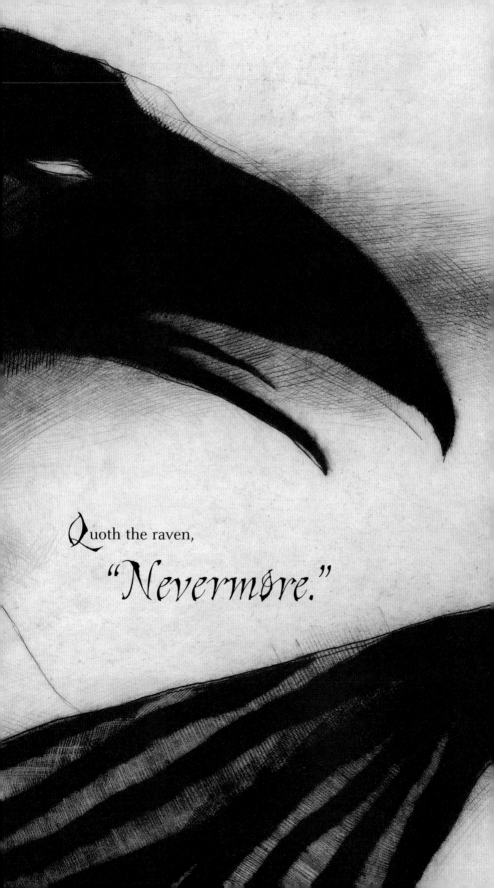

Quoth the raven,

"Nevermore."

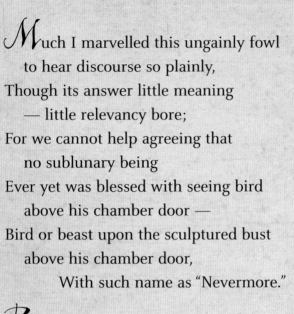

Much I marvelled this ungainly fowl
 to hear discourse so plainly,
Though its answer little meaning
 — little relevancy bore;
For we cannot help agreeing that
 no sublunary being
Ever yet was blessed with seeing bird
 above his chamber door —
Bird or beast upon the sculptured bust
 above his chamber door,
   With such name as "Nevermore."

But the raven, sitting lonely on the
 placid bust, spoke only
That one word, as if his soul in that
 one word he did outpour.
Nothing farther then he uttered
 — not a feather then he fluttered —
Till I scarcely more than muttered,
 "Other friends have flown before —
On the morrow *he* will leave,
 as my hopes have flown before."
  Quoth the raven,

"Nevermore."

*W*ondering at the stillness broken
　　by reply so aptly spoken,
"Doubtless," said I, "what it utters
　　is its only stock and store,
Caught from some unhappy master
　　whom unmerciful Disaster
Followed fast and followed faster
　　— so, when Hope he would adjure,
Stern Despair returned, instead of
　　the sweet Hope he dared adjure —
　　　That sad answer,

"Nevermore!"

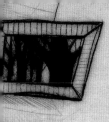

*B*ut the raven still beguiling all my
  sad soul into smiling,
Straight I wheeled a cushioned seat
  in front of bird, and bust, and door;
Then upon the velvet sinking,
  I betook myself to linking
Fancy unto fancy, thinking what this
  ominous bird of yore —
What this grim, ungainly, ghastly, gaunt,
  and ominous bird of yore
    Meant in croaking

"Nevermore."

*T*his I sat engaged in guessing,
  but no syllable expressing
To the fowl whose fiery eyes now
  burned into my bosom's core;
This and more I sat divining,
  with my head at ease reclining
On the cushion's velvet lining
  that the lamplight gloated o'er,
But whose velvet violet lining
  with the lamplight gloating o'er,
    She shall press, ah, nevermore!

$\mathcal{T}$hen, methought, the air grew denser,
  perfumed from an unseen censer

Swung by angels whose faint foot-falls
   tinkled on the tufted floor.
"Wretch," I cried, "thy God hath lent thee
   — by these angels he hath sent thee
Respite — respite and Nepenthe from
   thy memories of Lenore!
Let me quaff this kind Nepenthe
   and forget this lost Lenore!"
      Quoth the raven,

"*Nevermore.*"

"Prophet!" said I, "thing of evil!
   — prophet still, if bird or devil! —
Whether Tempter sent, or whether
   tempest tossed thee here ashore,
Desolate, yet all undaunted,
   on this desert land enchanted —
On this home by Horror haunted
   — tell me truly, I implore —
Is there — *is* there balm in Gilead?
   — tell me — tell me, I implore!"
Quoth the raven,

"Nevermore."

"Prophet!" said I, "thing of evil!
  — prophet still, if bird or devil!
By that Heaven that bends above us
  — by that God we both adore —
Tell this soul with sorrow laden if,
  within the distant Aidenn,
It shall clasp a sainted maiden
  whom the angels name Lenore —
Clasp a rare and radiant maiden
  whom the angels name Lenore."

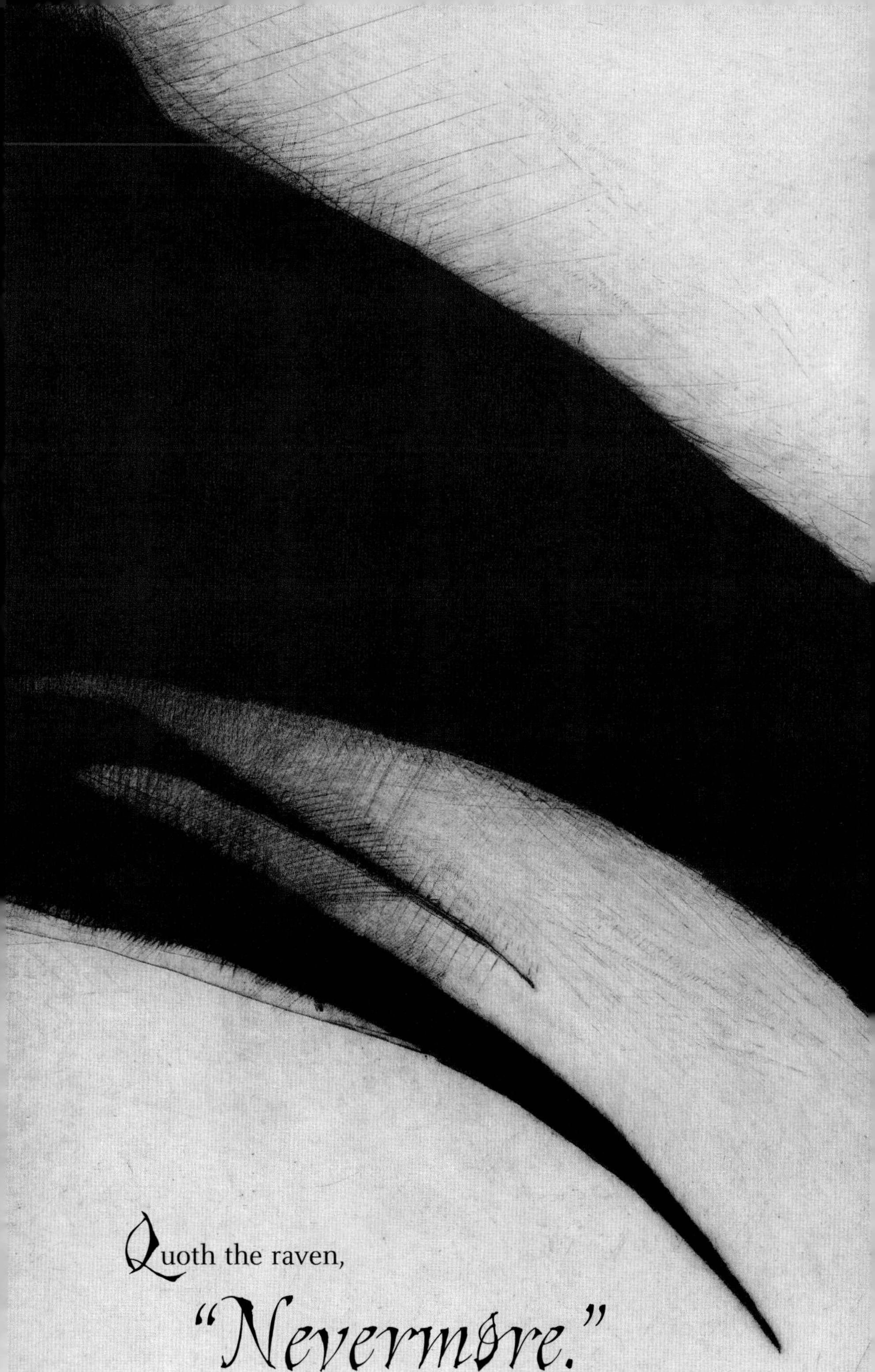

Quoth the raven,

"*Nevermore.*"

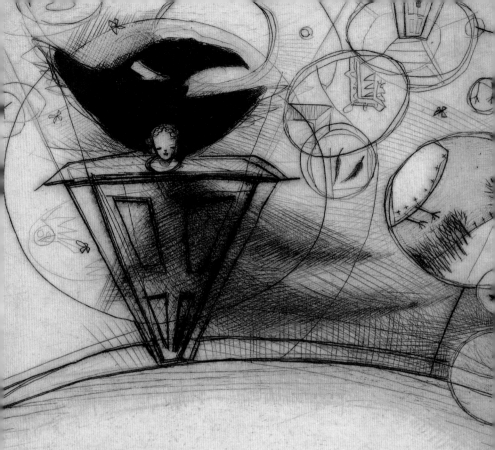

"Be that word our sign of parting,
   bird or fiend!" I shrieked, upstarting —
"Get thee back into the tempest
   and the Night's Plutonian shore!
Leave no black plume as a token
   of that lie thy soul hath spoken!
Leave my loneliness unbroken
   — quit the bust above my door!
Take thy beak from out my heart,
   and take thy form from off my door!"
     Quoth the raven,

        "Nevermore."

And the raven, never flitting,
 still is sitting, still is sitting
On the pallid bust of Pallas
 just above my chamber door;
And his eyes have all the seeming
 of a demon that is dreaming,
And the lamplight o'er him streaming
 throws his shadow on the floor;
And my soul from out that shadow
 that lies floating on the floor
 Shall be lifted —

nevermore!

Edgar Allan Poe

Few writers in the English language have left a legacy like that of American Edgar Allan Poe (1809–1849). Renowned for his short stories, poetry and literary criticism, Poe is also credited as the originator of the modern mystery or detective novel and as having a significant impact on science fiction, horror and gothic literature. Many believe the intriguing macabre and psychological elements of Poe's works were inspired by his own tortured life — his being orphaned at the age of two, his bouts with poverty, alcoholism and mental instability as well as the premature death of his young wife (a cousin whom he had married when she was only thirteen). Poe has been both hailed as a genius and denounced as a sub-literary vulgarian. Yet no one can deny the tremendous influence he has had upon generations of acclaimed writers, artists, composers and filmmakers, including Charles Baudelaire, Sir Arthur Conan Doyle, Jules Verne, Franz Kafka, Ray Bradbury, Gustave Doré, Sergei Rachmaninoff and Alfred Hitchcock.

Poe's international celebrity and reputation as a writer owe much to his best-known work, "The Raven." Often called the most famous American poem, it originally appeared in 1845 in the *New York Evening Mirror* and as the title piece in a collection published that same year. An eerily bleak narrative poem, "The Raven" delves into the hidden horrors of the human psyche as it traces a scholar's descent into madness, moving from sorrow over the loss of his beloved to jocularity, despair and eventually frenzied terror and the masochistic persecution of his own soul. In doing so, the poem explores with dramatic intensity the themes of remembrance, grief, guilt, obsession, instability and the human capacity for self-torture. With masterful use of such literary techniques as alliteration and repetition along with a hypnotic rhythm and rhyme scheme, Poe crafted one of the most disturbing and memorable poems of all time — one that has inspired countless other works of art and parodies, including a spoof on TV's *The Simpsons*. Will there ever be another poem that haunts the imagination as powerfully as Poe's "The Raven"? The answer, surely, is "Nevermore."

Ryan Price

Looking at the art of Ryan Price is like peering through a keyhole into the dark world of Edgar Allan Poe. But despite the pair's similar gothic sensibility and shared fascination with the oddities of human nature, Price discovered that illustrating "The Raven," his first book, was no easy task. First there was the challenge of depicting a long poem in which almost nothing happens. Then there was the difficulty of bringing this classic to life for a modern audience — one that might be unmoved by the poem's archaic language and Poe's near-clichéd raven, embedded as it is in popular culture, considered no more disturbing than Frankenstein's monster.

The key to the first puzzle came from Price's sense of the narrator's guilt. This led him to a create a background story for the characters via old photographs that hint at the narrator's involvement in Lenore's death and suggest, through associations between his bird-like frame and the raven's human-like form, that the fiendish fowl is really a manifestation of the narrator's guilt-ridden soul.

To make the poem more immediate and compelling for the twenty-first century reader, Price emphasized the most frightening elements of the verse, such as the narrator's slide into dementia, culminating in the final, terrifying illustration of the narrator imprisoned within the raven-like shadow he has scrawled around him. The intense blacks, the feathery quality of the images and the "ghosts" of old lines that are the result of Price's drypoint technique reinforce the chilling atmosphere. But it is also his quirky, black humor, evident in Lenore's floating form, and contemporary touches, such as the raven's elegant suit and television appearance, that will resonate with readers today. Indeed, this riveting, unsettling interpretation of Poe's classic will stay with us forevermore, much like that "grim, ungainly, ghastly, gaunt and ominous bird of yore."

Ryan Price is a fine artist and printmaker whose work has been widely exhibited. He has also illustrated editorial pieces as well as book and CD covers. Price lives in Guelph, Ontario, with his family.

To Andrea now; Ruby, Jack and Charley later;
and all my amazing families always.
With thanks to Tara, Karen, Kathe
and, most especially, Nadine — R.P.

The illustrations for this book were rendered in a medium called
"drypoint printmaking." Drypoint is similar to etching, but involves
working an image with various tools (instead of acid) onto a copper plate,
which is then inked and run through a printing press.

The text was set in

Celeste and *Aspera*

⌗

KCP Poetry is an imprint of Kids Can Press

Illustrations © 2006 Ryan Price

Kids Can Press acknowledges the financial support of the Government of Ontario,
through the Ontario Media Development Corporation's Ontario Book Initiative;
the Ontario Arts Council; the Canada Council for the Arts; and
the Government of Canada, through the BPIDP, for our publishing activity.

Published in Canada by   Published in the U.S. by
Kids Can Press Ltd.   Kids Can Press Ltd.
29 Birch Avenue   2250 Military Road
Toronto, ON M4V 1E2   Tonawanda, NY 14150

www.kidscanpress.com

Edited by Tara Walker
Designed by Karen Powers
Printed and bound in China

This book is smyth sewn casebound.

CM 06 0 9 8 7 6 5 4 3 2 1

Library and Archives Canada Cataloguing in Publication

Poe, Edgar Allan, 1809–1849.
The raven / Edgar Allan Poe ; illustrated by Ryan Price.

(Visions in poetry)

ISBN-13: 978-1-55337-473-2   ISBN-10: 1-55337-473-8

1. Children's poetry, American.   2. Fantasy poetry, American.
I. Price, Ryan, 1972– II. Title. III. Series.

PS2609.A1 2006   j811'.3   C2005-906798-5

Kids Can Press is a **l©ɾʊs**™ Entertainment company